Set Free to Stay Free
by
Jean West

Unless otherwise indicated, all scriptural quotations are from the Authorized King James Version of the Bible.

Scripture quotations marked (MSG) are taken from The Message. Copyright © 1993, 1994, 1995, 1996, 2000, 2001, 2002. Used by permission of NavPress Publishing Group.

Copyright © 2015 by Jean West

First printing October 2015

ISBN-13: 978-1517562953

ISBN-10: 1517562953

Razor Wire Photography by Robin Overacre

Cover Design by Sandi Bird Aldridge

Published by:

Audeamus Publications

PO Box 784

New Castle, VA 24127

www.audeamuspublications.com

All rights reserved by the author. No part of this book may be reproduced in any form or by any electronic or mechanical means, including information storage and retrieval systems, except for the inclusion of brief quotations in a review, without express permission in writing from the authors or their representative.

In Loving Memory Of...

...Pastor Margaret L. Bass, my mother, who knew I had good intentions to write this book. She did not get to see it to fruition; however, she was determined to see my son "set free" and reconnected with our family, and God gave her the desires of her heart. My mother's last words of wisdom to my son was *(this is my paraphrase)* "June, stay on the straight and narrow path and don't go back...you promise?" He replied, "I promise, Grandma."

Dedication

I dedicate this book to some extremely special people in my life. To Sister Barbara who saw something in my testimony that I didn't see, and hence planted the seed in my heart to write this book. Thanks for believing in me.

To my awesome husband, whom I absolutely cherish as my gift from God. Thanks for your continual love and support encouraging me to keep moving forward with this assignment. Surely God knew everything I would need when He created you just for me. I love you, honey.

To Shone, Junior *(hereinafter referred to as June–short for Junior)*, and my grandchildren, Tayonna, Trey and Jonathan, I am blessed among woman to have such precious jewels. You guys are my glow of sunshine, and the biggest smile on my face. I am very proud of you all–hugs and kisses.

From the depths of my heart, I value all of you for being my steady rock to hold onto when I thought for sure at times that the earth would surely swallow me up. I love all of you from the bottom of heart.

The Spirit of the Lord God is upon me;

because the Lord

Hath anointed me to preach good tidings

unto the meek; He hath sent me

to bind up the brokenhearted,

to proclaim liberty to the captives,

*and the opening of the **prison** to them that are bound;*

Isaiah 61:1

Table of Contents

Dedication 1

In the Beginning 5

Transfers and Displacement 11

The Outcome 17

Another Hard Hit 25

Visitations by Family and Friends 31

Close Calls 41

Blessed By Kairos Weekends 47

Sharing My Story at Church 57

The Journey Home 63

About The Author 71

Chapter 1

In the Beginning

"³Lo, children are an heritage of the LORD: and the fruit of the womb is his reward." ~ Psalms 127:3. I am in total agreement with this scripture—children are absolutely a wonderful blessing and an extension of who you are as a parent and as a person. I have two wonderful children, Shone and June *(short for Junior)*, and three grandchildren, Tayonna, Trey, and Jonathan, all of whom I hold dear and close to my heart.

Raising children is a tough job and a huge responsibility to face up to, but in my opinion, it's so worth it. No matter how many children are in a household, the mother is usually the CEO in charge. She is constantly coaching the children, teaching them, and training them how to be an asset to society, to be successful while maintaining integrity, and, most importantly, how to eventually leave their nest with ease of flight and accomplish a safe landing in life.

You stand on the sidelines being a cheerleader for your children, pointing them towards the right target, because you want them to have a better life than you had; so, in turn, each generation progresses to a higher level. Then in the midst of all of your efforts, a metamorphosis takes place right before your eyes, and your children begin to change a little each day as the years zoom by. The next thing you know, it seems as though you blink your eyes once or twice, and poof, they're all grown up.

At this point, most parents' dream would be that all is well with their adult children because they have done the best job they could possibly do throughout each stage of their children's lives, with the hope they will advance and go much further than could ever be imagined. I know I didn't do everything right, but I did what I thought was best at the time.

One would think that it's time to take a deep cleansing breath as you watch them enter the career world, get married, and hopefully have children of their own. But just as I was about to do that…and maybe pick a few flowers along my path, everything came to a screeching halt when my son made a really bad decision; as a result, he was sentenced to prison for a number of years. This book is my testimony about how God elevated me above the storm of my son's incarceration and gave me great peace in the midst of all the ugly and uncomfortable details that went along with it.

No one, including myself wants to talk about something like this, especially when you are a Christian and raised your children in the church all of their lives. Nevertheless, stuff happens in Christians' lives too. There is no exception to the rule; however, the difference is that we are more than conquerors. And by overcoming each challenge, God blesses us to be a blessing to others; to that end, I had to drop my pride, guilt, and embarrassment so that this book could be written. My prayer is that you will see the incredible love that God continuously pours out upon His people no matter what happens.

First, I'll tell you a little bit about my son. He was a smart student in elementary school, clever, and good at learning things quickly. June is a talented musician, and in high school he was voted most likely to succeed among his peers. He served in the United States Air Force and received an honorable discharge. What I most appreciate about June is his sense of humor, because he will keep you laughing. Most of our family gatherings are eventually centered around him cracking jokes on his sister; she then retaliates with a funny story about him – one that has an even greater punchline, and they go back and forth. It is absolutely hilarious, but "ya gotta be there" to really get it. In a nutshell, he is the "life of the party" type of guy. He loves dogs, is very outgoing and finds it easy to make friends. June has always been extremely close to his sister and still is. I Thank God for my son and our strong family.

It is extremely difficult for me to think back to the beginning of this story because it brings up such bad memories, but in the same vein, it is also therapeutic to share it with the express intent to bless and encourage another family who may already have a loved one in prison or be poised at the brink of their loved one being sent to prison.

The pain intensified itself because my thoughts were, "How and why did this happen?" We took our children to church, on vacations, summer camps, participated in school functions, years of piano lessons, and other wholesome activities that should have produced a young man who did not go to prison; but it happened anyway.

So what do you do? I'm glad you asked. The only thing you can do is pick yourself up, dust yourself off, and move forward to do what must be done whatever that may be at the time. For me, I *on purpose* chose to continue to trust God more than at any time before, and allowed Him to guide me through the mess of having my son incarcerated for a number of years.

I had asked God a long time ago to save my son; however, when he ended up in prison, I wanted to have a conference with God to inform Him that this was definitely *NOT* what I had in mind. I told God, "This situation is not looking good, and what in world am I going to do?" My son was in deep trouble and there was no way I could come up with the money to hire a good attorney to defend him – within my soul I screamed, 'God help me!' The next item on the list was a total blank because I had no plan "B". Many times I felt so helpless, because I was unable to turn things around. It appeared that everything I could do wasn't good enough, and I felt like I was traveling around in a thick fog with my faith in God being my only comfort.

My son's case was highly publicized on the news, in the newspaper, and on the radio. It seemed like I had been thrown into an F-5 tornado without any type of shelter and no way of escape. The only way I can explain how I felt when everything was happening in the beginning is to quote a familiar saying, "I didn't know whether I was coming or going." I'd had a sickening knot in the pit of my stomach that would not release its hold.

Close friends would call me after they heard about the situation by word of mouth or from the media; for a while, I refused to answer the phone. I made the choice to not discuss the matter with them face-to-face, other than to briefly say yes, it was my son, and kept it moving. But after approximately six months, I could talk a little bit about it. The publicity finally died down, the dust settled, and I was still standing—imagine that.

I would think at times that maybe I was having a really bad nightmare, and hopefully I would soon wake up and everything would be back to normal. June would be home with the family, and I could breathe again without feeling like my heart was crushed into a million pieces. Unfortunately, instead of being an awful nightmare, it was an awful reality. Every facet of June's incarceration was, indeed, real; it was painful, it was embarrassing, and I did not want to go through this ordeal—but I had to move beyond my emotions.

By the grace of God, He fixed my mind so I could walk this thing out. That meant listening to the good—and sometimes not so good—comments from family members, the whispering at church, and the really bad reports from the media. I remember asking God how I would be able to get through this; He answered by asking me, "How do you get through anything else?" I answered, "One day at a time," and His reply was, "Then start marking each day off on your calendar. While doing so, say to yourself, "My son is one day closer to home, rather than being further away." Eventually, just by mixing those words with that action, I gained a second wind for each day, week, and month as the years went by.

I cried and prayed for a miracle of early release for my son every year; but God knew in His infinite wisdom that early release would not resolve the core issue inside June, because he needed to receive a total healing of his spirit, soul and body. So I didn't get a "yes" to that particular prayer—which is what I wanted so badly, but I did receive peace and strength for each day from my heavenly Father.

Chapter 2

Transfers and Displacement

Surprisingly, June called me at work to tell me he was being picked up and taken to the city jail. I heard him trying to say more but the phone was abruptly hung up by the police officer. I was nearly hysterical with fear, so I left my desk and went into an empty office for privacy, and called a dear friend at my church whom I knew to be trustworthy. She not only listened to my awful story, but immediately she and her husband loaned me the money to bail him out.

June was out for only 24 hours. The next morning they picked him up again and he was at the city jail for one day, then onto a county jail for 11 months. While he was there, visitation time was only 20 minutes, and I had to talk to him through a small opening at the bottom of a thick glass wall. Though the barrier stood between us, we always greeted each other by simultaneously placing one hand on the glass as a point of contact.

In the beginning I knew he was scared because he would constantly ring his hands and say, "Ma, I don't think I can do this! These people are crazy in here...I'm *NOT* supposed to be here." Then in the next breath he began spilling out all the happenings of that week, court rulings, arguments between the inmates, etc. Looking at him and hearing what he said made me feel extremely uneasy, but I couldn't do anything about it.

On one particular visit, my daughter was with me. She was listening to her brother's words, observing the expressions on his face, and then intentionally kept a close watch on how I was taking everything in. When the visit was over she said, "Ma, June is nervous and scared, but he will be alright." I said, "You think so?" She said, "Yes, I'm sure of it." Those words comforted my soul, held back Niagara Falls from streaming down my face, and redirected my thinking to agree with her point of view... Yeah, he'll be alright even though he didn't look like it, and he definitely didn't sound like it.

June made friends with a guy who had been there for about two years. So my son asked him: How do you do it–surviving day in and day out being locked up? I will never forget what the man's reply was. He said, "When you feel like you're at the end of your rope, tie a knot at the end of it and hang on." I don't know who benefited more from that statement, me or my son, but June caught hold of that vision; it enabled him to hang in there and settle his mind to some extent. After June told me about his conversation with his new friend, he felt better, and I did too.

One evening he called me and said, "Ma, I got some good news." Although I couldn't imagine what kind of good news he had under the circumstances, curiosity overruled my doubts as I said, "What?" He went on to tell me how he felt so distraught that he actually knelt down at his cot and began to pray and cry out to God in a loud voice. June said he prayed until all the other inmates and the guards got quiet. He prayed until the Holy Spirit overshadowed him and he spoke in tongues without concern for the length of time spent in prayer or what others thought about him. He prayed and prayed and prayed some more, until, when he had finished praying, everything he had on was drenched in sweat. He'd managed to pull himself up on his cot and went to sleep.

He said with great joy, "Ma, I got the Holy Ghost that night!" I was truly happy for June, and I wanted him to have this experience, but I kept thinking to myself, *why in jail?* Then I heard God whisper to me, "He had to be in jail to have a desperate enough need to seek my face." I knew that was the truth and nothing but the truth.

Even when we bring calamity upon our own lives through bad decisions or whatever the case may be, no matter what the results or penalty of that bad decision is, if you seek God's face, He will hear your prayer and help you. The help might not be what you wanted or how you wanted it, but its help just the same. Thank God for His mercy and forgiveness; nevertheless, June had to reap what he had sown. At least now he had the spiritual power to endure what was ahead of him which was a long hard road.

I must admit, at that time I had not accepted the fact that June would actually have to pull all of the time given to him, because I was praying for the miracle of early release or at least a short term detention camp. As a matter of fact, June's probation officer did recommend a detention camp to the judge and the judge approved it. June took the physical exam in preparation for the detention camp.

He was given a list of certain clothing items and toiletries he was required to pack and we thought, *This is good, this will work.* But unfortunately, the prosecutor objected and the decision was overturned while our court appointed attorney basically sat there and did nothing. It was just a set up. I know that now, but I didn't know it then.

Okay, at that point June was telling me that his fellow inmates told him to hire a real attorney to enter a motion to change the complexion of the charges, and they also gave the name of a very prominent attorney who could possibly help us. I contacted the attorney and left several messages before his extremely busy schedule *finally* allowed him to return my call. We talked briefly about the case, which he was to some extent familiar with because of the high media exposure. He agreed to enter the motion on June's behalf provided we could come up with his fee.

We rallied together as a family, pulling money from a couple of different directions, and finally collected enough for the attorney's fee. When the court date arrived, we had five good, credible witnesses who were all willing and ready to testify on my son's behalf. We were prepped by the attorney a few minutes before court convened. I didn't feel as rattled as before, and I was expecting a good outcome. Our hopes were up and our day in court was here.

Unfortunately, the prosecutor objected to the motion—claiming he wasn't prepared, then he proceeded to review all of the charges again to the point I just felt outdone and very disappointed. What we set out to accomplish went down the drain in a split second, but at least I knew I had done everything possible.

June called me that evening still being hopeful that someway somehow there was maybe at least one more rock could be overturned in an effort to swing some evidence in his favor. I heard it in his voice when he said, "Okay ma, what's the next step – what are we gonna do next?" I remember mustering up enough energy to say in a very easy-going shallow tone of voice, "There is no next step, June. That was it." There was a devastating silence on the phone, then he said, "Okay ma. I gotta go." We usually talked for the entire 15 minutes allotted and sometimes he would call me again to talk some more, but not that night.

My description of that particular conversation is…it pierced my heart to the core. The conversation was very short because there was really nothing else to say. I felt his pain as we both realized he faced a dead end street.

Chapter 3

The Outcome

The day of sentencing came as a thief in the night and was a dark day for the family. While sitting there focused, my heart pounding with a surge of anxiety, I began to see little bits of folded paper drop in my lap and onto the floor but I ignored them. The same thing was happening to Shone but she picked up one of the small pieces of paper, unraveled it, read it, and realized it was verses from the Bible. Alarmed, Shone leaned forward and whispered, "Ma, this woman behind us is throwing tiny, folded-up scriptures at us. I quickly held my hand up giving her the stop signal and whispered back to her, "I don't have time for that, because I don't want to miss what the judge is gonna say."

When I said that, Shone reluctantly

leaned back into her seat – but she was hot as a fire cracker at the nerve of this woman who was harassing us. Come to find out the woman came to court in support of the plaintiff but decided to sit on our side for the sole purpose to mock and insult us, because she knew we were Christians. Who does that? I wondered why anyone would use Bible scriptures to point a finger and try to smash someone else when we've all been guilty of something at one time or another. What can I say? I chose to ignore the woman, but Shone didn't.

Finally, all the facts had been laid out and testimonies heard, but before the judge gave his sentence, he looked at me and assured me that he had read all of the recommendation letters that had been sent in on behalf of June. Then he looked at June and said, "You've not only broken the law but you've gone against your upbringing." I will never forget those earsplitting words despite the truth they contained. The judge gave his sentence; he didn't give June the maximum penalty, because he was a first time offender. Of course, it was still more time than we expected or wanted.

Then it came, the awful strike of the gavel on the sounding block which indicated court was adjourned. *'It's over, it's done?'* I asked myself, *'Really?'* Yes, really. As we stood up the woman behind us made a sneering remark to deliberately display her approval of the sentence – like a flash of lightening Shone made an attempt to leap over the bench to shut this woman up once and for all, but thankfully, a brother from our church was able to hold her back. "Sis," he said in a very calming tone of voice, "don't do it. It's not worth it." He had a good grip on her, but Shone dared the woman to say something else in an extremely threatening tone of voice! "Go ahead! I dare you to say something else!" she spewed.

Evidently the woman in question realized Shone would make good on her threat so she got out of that courtroom with a quickness. Okay, at this point I'm just done with the sentence, and the episode with Shone and the stranger. All I could think was, *'Oh my God! If Shone jumps on this woman, **both** of my kids are going to jail today...'* Thankfully, Shone got herself together a little bit, but she was still steaming.

They allowed June to be with us for about two minutes. I was crying. Shone was crying. Family and friends encircled June, hugging him and giving words of encouragement. But for some reason I never did get a chance to hug him or say anything. Standing there looking at him with everyone else around him, I felt like I was stuck in mud and couldn't get out.

Overwhelmed with compassion, my wheels were spinning but for some unknown reason I just couldn't get to him. I never got close enough to give him a hug or say any words. In my heart I somehow sensed a feeling of guilt, not for committing any crime...but as a parent. Even recalling that day makes me sigh deeply and shake my head with flashes of sadness.

Just before the guards took him away, my daughter asked if they would please take the handcuffs off so they could hug each other. The guard said, "No," so with hands cuffed and feet chained, June took two hops towards his sister and laid his head upon her shoulder. She embraced him for a moment, then they took him away. Shone told me about that later because I didn't see him do that, and I was thankful I didn't. I'm sure God was shielding my eyes and my ears because He knew I had been through enough for one day.

The guards took him and at times I can still hear the rattle of clanking chains hitting the pavement with each step he took. June was taken back into the courthouse in a room with a window that faced the street and fortunately we could see him. I walked over to the window and mouthed "I love you" as I watched the tears stream down his face, he said the same thing to me as he waved goodbye. I turned away from the window and we left to head back home.

It was only a 45 minute trip back to Roanoke but it seemed like a long, mind-numbing stretch across a hot desert. Shone burst into tears and I was crying too. I don't remember what, if anything, I said to console her, because my own heart was crushed. For the most part we were pretty much both jacked-up. Finally we arrived at the babysitter's house *(I will refer to her as Barbara)*, because we had to pick up Trey, Shone's son. She looked at us and asked why the down faces, so I briefly told her what happened in court.

All of a sudden, to my surprise, Barbara looked at me with her head poked through the opened window and began to declare in a loud commanding voice "**MY SISTER, WE STILL HAVE THE VICTORY! WE HAVE THE VICTORY!!!**" I was so hungry for a word from heaven, I said to her, "Say it again, Barbara!" She stood straight and tall and declared again, "**WE HAVE THE VICTORY! WE HAVE THE VICTORY!!!**"

Shone didn't get what she meant so, after securing Trey into his car seat, she quickly pulled out of Barbara's driveway. She couldn't see how anyone could make a statement like that when her brother was just sentenced to prison for a long time. To tell you the truth my "head" didn't wrap around it either, but my spirit-man knew exactly what she was talking about. And for those few moments, my heart was lifted as my eyes were glued to Barbara dancing in her driveway, praising God and still saying "**WE HAVE THE VICTORY! WE HAVE THE VICTORY!!!**" It was a sight for sore eyes to see someone praising God even though I didn't have the strength to join her.

Barbara's high praise was my special gift that day as I continued to watch her through the rear window until I couldn't see her anymore. That scene brings to my mind the scripture that says *"[1]It is a good thing to give thanks unto the LORD, and to sing praises unto thy name, O most High: [2]To shew forth thy lovingkindness in the morning, and thy faithfulness every night,"* ~ Psalms 92:1-2. In hindsight, I understand now that we really did have the victory, which was the truth in God's eyesight, but "time" had to catch up with the truth.

In other words, neither my daughter nor I could see the benefit of what had happened, but God works a thing out from the end to beginning – we, however, don't think like that. We see what we see, hear what we hear and usually don't go too far past those facts. That's where faith comes in to keep you steady.

June stayed at the county jail for a few more weeks then without any notice to the family, he was moved to another facility. Another transfer, another displacement.

He was transferred to Mecklenburg which was 3 ½ hours away from Roanoke. But at least we would be able to hug him after almost a year. He settled in and of course made a friend with his roommate. Our first visit with him was very much like a party. We hugged him, laughed and talked for a couple of hours, then the visit was over. Shone and I visited him there several times. Just when we had the trip down pat, he was transferred.

Fortunately, somehow June got wind of the transfer and was able to tell me in advance not to visit him so I wouldn't waste the gas and my day, which made me a very happy camper. He was there for only 6 months and when he left his friend got up with him early that morning and fixed him breakfast, which consisted of a cup of hot chocolate and a pack of Ramon Noodles – considered a gourmet meal behind bars.

That one act of kindness went a long way with my son, and encouraged his heart to know that God would bless him through other people no matter where he was. It's called the favor God. When June told me that story it was absolutely inspiring and was the best part of my day.

The next facility was Augusta Correctional Center where he remained for a total of five years. He had a couple of jobs there, one being a teacher's assistant helping the guys obtain their GED, and the other one was working in the kitchen, which was an awesome advantage because it enabled him to eat the fresh food which was given to the officers. He could eat as much as he wanted because kitchen workers got first dibs. As usual, unfortunately, the rotten stale food was served to the other inmates.

June told me his first day on the job, he ate so much his stomach was on stuffed mode for hours. The other kitchen workers told him, "Take it easy man. Don't make yourself sick!" They laughed, probably remembering that they did the same thing when they first got the job. The rule was you could eat all you wanted, but you couldn't take any food back to your cell. If they caught you stealing food your job was gone, so June followed orders, burped and patted his full belly back to his cell every day.

He found out this facility had thriving weekly church services, and he quickly put in a request to be in attendance. One particular officer gave him a really hard time two or three times, claiming his paperwork wasn't in order; because of that, he wouldn't allow him to attend the church service. June didn't like it but he managed to maintain his peace and proceeded to walk back to his cell. On his way back, another officer saw him walking in the opposite direction from where the service was being held.

He asked June, "I thought you were going to church?" June explained what had happened, and the officer's reply was, "No one should be denied a chance to go to church."

Being a sergeant, he was able to sign off on June's paperwork. When June turned around again for the third time in an attempt to go to church, the first officer saw June and started yelling, "Didn't I tell you: no stamped pass, no attendance. What part of that don't you understand?" June calmly handed him the paperwork signed by the sergeant. The officer turned red because he had not only thought his papers weren't in order, but due to the fact that a higher ranking officer had signed June's papers on short notice, he had no other alternative but to step aside and allow him to attend church. That was good news!

Chapter 4

Another Hard Hit

June was finally settled in and going to church on a weekly basis; he had been a resident at Augusta Correctional Center for about two years. Suddenly, another blow comes down the pike. The plaintiffs had just decided that they wanted to file for punitive damages to the tune of one million dollars. It was ridiculous, because that document was supposed to be attached to their original Complaint but it wasn't. Punitive damages are damages exceeding simple compensation and awarded to punish the defendant.

I felt like it was all a scheme to continuously keep this case in the public's eye, and, to add insult to injury, this new information was posted in the newspaper on the front page. I didn't even know about it until someone at my church brought it to my attention in an effort to give me a heads-up. I was thankful that they did, so I could try and figure out what my next move would be.

Immediately, the court papers were mailed directly to my son in prison, and my head was in complete turmoil. This stunt was legally improper because you cannot sue a minor, a deceased person or someone who is incarcerated; for obvious reasons they are unable to defend themselves in any way. When my son called me explaining the documents he had received in the mail, I knew he needed an attorney…but the fact was I didn't have the money to pay for one.

Feeling helpless, I prayed, and begged God to just make all of this stuff go away, but in a real world it didn't. Fear overwhelmed my heart, but despite the fact of being afraid, I also knew something had to be done as soon as possible. I called the attorney who represented my son on a previous matter, and asked him what his retainer fee would be to represent June on the punitive damages issue. He quoted a fee of $30,000.00. That figure was certainly not in my budget, so I had to start searching for help elsewhere as time was quickly passing, and I did not want the papers to go into default. Default means failure to perform a legal duty, such as filing your responsive document in court within the 21 day time limit.

Sitting at my desk, on my job which just happened to be at a law firm, I decided to call an attorney who had resigned from the firm. I didn't want my business spread all over the office. She listened to my dilemma, gave me some uplifting words and then advised me that she could not help me because she was not a criminal attorney. She then asked me if I had talked to the attorney for whom I worked, Brian, about the case and I said, "No." Her tone became very serious as she strongly advised me to talk to Brian immediately. After speaking with this attorney, I was able to wipe my tears, gained courage from her tender words and walked into Brian's office to speak with him.

Still shaking on the inside, I began to tell him the story about my son and how I needed his help to defend him. I will never forget the blank look on his face as he interrupted me and said, "Wait a minute! Jean, where did the incident happen?" I gave him the location of the incident, all while thinking in my mind oh my goodness now what?

Then Brian said these words to me which hit me like a ton of bricks, "Jean, that case is already in this office, it was assigned to me and I cannot help you because I represent the other defendant." However, he went on to say, "But what I can do for you is dictate a Motion to Dismiss the papers because they were improperly served upon your son without him having legal representation."

My next question was how I could get an attorney to represent my son, to which Brian explained that the court would appoint a Guardian ad Litem which is a fancy term for a court appointed attorney to protect the legal interest of a minor or a person unable to defend himself due to incarceration. Well at this point I'm starting to feel a little bit better. However, Brian advised me that before he could do anything he would have to get permission from the head partner. He said he would speak to the partner first, and then call me back into his office. I left Brian's office praying each and every step back to my desk.

After a short time, Brian buzzed me to join him and the partner in his office. The partner sympathized with me and gave Brian permission to do whatever he could to assist me and my son until a Guardian ad Litem was appointed. Furthermore, the partner assured me that even though the case was in the office, the confidentiality of the matter would be kept and no one else would know except me, Brian and himself.

Just before the meeting ended, the partner asked me, "Jean, since Brian is assigned to this case and it involves your son, will you be up to the task of working on this file?" I remember my exact words, I looked him straight in his eyes and said, "Yes, because I am a professional." Right at that juncture, I had a perfect opportunity to say I did not want to work on my son's file, but why would I pass up the opportunity to oversee each stage of the case; and more importantly, I couldn't pass up the opportunity to bathe it with prayer every time I worked on the file.

The partner smiled at me and said he understood my efforts to do everything I could do to help my son. He also said, "If it were one of his children, I would do the same thing." Brian agreed whole heartedly – their words were very soothing.

I prayed for a quick settlement every day, and Brian did as much as he could on the case, but finally he had to advise the judge that his secretary was the mother of one of the defendants, and that he had drafted all the previous papers for me so that June would not be in default. The judge told Brian it was alright with him and that he understood his concern in trying to assist me. Of course, I know the judge could have objected, but thank God his attitude towards Brian helping me was one more powerful move of God's favor on my behalf.

Now comes some more really good news. The court finally appointed a Guardian ad Litem to represent my son's interest in the case, and guess who the court appointed? The exact same attorney who told me his fee would be $30,000.00. Yes indeed! God granted me the desires of my heart because he was the one I wanted in the first place, but now I had his services free of charge.

Look at God! Isn't He awesome? When I had the opportunity, I asked the attorney how he got appointed to June's case. He said, "I knew what the prosecuting attorney was going to do to your son, so I volunteered to represent him." As I fought back tears, I expressed my deep gratitude for his services and thanked him over and over again. In addition to that blessing, when all of the liens and/or claims of punitive liability were released from the other defendants, they were released off of June as well.

I give God all the credit for helping me take one step at a time walking by faith and not by sight, which ultimately lifted me to new levels of courage and strength that I would have never known without the choice I made to trust Him. In Deuteronomy 30:19b, it says, *"...that I have set before you life and death, blessing and cursing: therefore choose life, that both thou and thy seed may live:"* I am convinced the choices we make and the words we speak over our lives will form our future for the good or bad, whether we know this truth or not.

Chapter 5

Visitations by Family and Friends

My daughter and I visited June at each and every correctional facility he spent time in, because love will always go the last mile and then some. When she had to work, I went alone. It didn't matter if it was snow, rain, or fog, I still went to see about him – but I was most thankful for the clear sunny days.

The very first time my daughter and I went to visit June at the third facility, we noticed that people were purchasing snacks to enjoy with their love one they came to visit. We didn't know you could bring quarters to buy snacks so we just sat there waiting for June to be released so he could be with us in the visitation area.

While waiting, a lady who spoke somewhat

broken English asked us in her own way if we had quarters, and we said, "No." She then put her hands together to form a cup. She looked at me as if to say, "You do the same," so I made a cup with my hands not realizing what her intentions were.

Then this precious woman reached into her bag that was filled with quarters and poured an abundance of money into my cupped hands, to the point of overflow. Shone and I were so blessed and amazed that this woman wanted to share what she had with us so we could buy snacks too. We said thank you quite a few times, and her only response was, "You keep…you keep for your visit." When June finally came to where we were, we told him what happened and his heart was blessed also as we ate snacks, drank cold soft drinks and just enjoyed each other's company.

On a couple occasions my girlfriend Christine would come with me to visit June, do the driving, and afterwards treat me to lunch. That was a blast! I appreciated the historical tour Christine took me on because she went to college in Lexington which was right next door to Staunton, Virginia where June was. She also faithfully sent him birthday and Christmas cards every year and Sudoku puzzles to keep his mind occupied.

I am eternally grateful for my good friends and family who supported me by taking the trip with me. On one occasion I had both of my girlfriends in the car with me going to visit June and both of them had the name Christine. We laughed and talked about a bunch of stuff *(as girls do)* and had a lot of fun that uplifted my very soul. Even though it took an hour and a half each way, that day, it didn't matter because my girlfriends had sacrificed their entire day on a Saturday to be with me and June, so the trip that day was much shorter.

Sometimes I had my car filled with my grandchildren, Tayonna, Trey, and Jonathan. Tayonna was an awesome help because the boys were toddlers at the time, and on the way back stopping at McDonald's for lunch was one of the highlights of our day. But on one very memorable occasion Tracie *(my niece)* traveled from Richmond to join Shone and myself to see June. This being her first time she wanted to know beforehand, did he still have his crazy sense of humor and would he be in chains. I assured her his spirits were high, and no he would not be in chains.

When June came out, he was pleasantly surprised to see his cousin as he greeted all of us with hugs. We stayed a couple of hours talking and laughing about family memories until we were bent over the table trying not to be loud, and June was laughing so hard he was crying and almost fell out of his chair. We laughed until another resident sitting at the table next to ours turned around and said "Hey, I want to laugh too!" In response, it was all I could do to turn around, move my head from left to right and I managed to get out, "Nooo - I can't tell you what we're laughing about." He looked disappointed, but he got the message.

Then there was the time when my car needed some repair work done on it so I was unable to make the trip to visit June. So I began to fill up my Saturday morning with my regular chores, when suddenly I heard a knock on my door. It was a couple from the church, Frank and Shelly, and they asked me if I was going to visit June today. I said no and explained why. They looked at me with so much compassion and said aww, but if you had a car you would go see him...right? I said, "Yeah, of course." They said, "Well, we gotta go, but we just wanted to check on you," and they left.

About 15 minutes later Shelly called to advise me she and Frank were at Enterprise Car Rental, renting a car so I could see June. WOW! My heart was filled with joy because God had the right people, at the right time, set aside to do exactly what I needed done. I got ready for my trip and soon they were at my door again, handed me the keys to the car and money to refill the tank when I returned the car. I was so appreciative for their kindness and thoughtfulness towards me, knowing that God was using them as instruments in His mighty hands. How wonderful is that?

Then there were the special greetings through the mail when our church and close family members sent June letters, cards, pictures of church events, and money placed on his account so he could purchase the things he needed. At one point he had so many letters and cards that he would use them as a curtain for privacy when he wanted to pray. June told me he'd go to each man and ask him did they have a prayer request. If they did, he would write them down on his pad then go in his cell and very carefully began putting up his curtain of letters and cards using tape. When the bars to his cell were fully covered, he would pray. June told me the paper curtain going up was a signal to everyone else not to bother him because he was praying.

In my imagination, I could clearly see the paper wall and June on his knees praying to God on behalf of himself and his friends. So as he was praying there behind the wall, I was praying every chance I could get on the outside. I knew everything would work out for our good because the scripture says, *"...and pray one for another, that ye may be healed. The effectual fervent prayer of a righteous man availeth much."* ~ James 5:16

Another blessing was when Brother Karl from our church would enthusiastically lead a group of brothers for a Saturday visit to encourage June. The brothers would listen to his praise reports concerning his survival behind the wall, and talk "guy talk," whatever that is. Christian men who are willing to sacrifice the majority of their day on Saturday to inspire, encourage and exhort another brother who is in dire need of spiritual support is a powerful thing. In addition to that, they would ask June what he needed, and they would meet the need.

There is no challenge or problem a man can ever be faced with that can measure up to the strength that is gained from "brothers" supporting another "brother." Very powerful! However, as the years marched on those visits eventually phased out, and I asked God why. My answer was clear as crystal. God spoke to my heart and said, "Why are you expecting man to do what I am already doing. **I AM** VISITING YOUR SON, **I AM** COMFORTING HIM, **I AM** CLEANING HIM UP AND MAKING HIM FIT FOR MY USE; and if the brothers from the church continue to visit him on a monthly basis until he comes home, who will get the glory for keeping him encouraged?" With that answer my soul was totally satisfied. Right there at that point I caught a glimpse of God's handiwork in my life and in my son's life. God wanted me to rest in Him, trust Him, and have patience.

All that I had received from God that day was confirmed on my next visit with June. We were talking about his spiritual growth, among other things; and all of a sudden June said, "Ma, guess what happened to me the other day?" I said, "What?" He explained how he was looking out the window, pass the barbwire, pass the fence and focused on the beautiful mountains, and he said, "God, I want to go home," as one tear rolled down my face. Then he said, "Ma, right after I spoke those words — **I could actually feel the warmth of God's arms wrap around me, and he held me in His arms.**"

This unconditional love my son received from God during those precious moments gave him the strength he needed to make him feel totally restored just as if nothing had ever happened to disturb his peace. He went on to say, "Ma, after those moments of God embracing me, I was then able to walk away from the window with the assurance I would be alright." He said, "I even went into the pod and whipped my friend in a game of dominions!"

We laughed. As he shared his experience with me, I sat there amazed, trying to imagine what the arms of God must have felt like. After hearing a testimony like that, I knew beyond a shadow of a doubt that my answer from God was being manifested – not on a monthly basis – but on a daily basis just like He said. You can't get any better than that.

God had a ram in the bush to bring up the tail end of June's time served, and his name is Brother Ajay. Brother Ajay blessed June and me by his faithful annual visits for the remaining years. I don't know anyone else who would be willing to make a prison visit on such a big family holiday as New Year's Day, but Ajay did. He decided this was an excellent opportunity for him to tithe the time of his entire New Year by making the sacrifice to be on the road by 7:00 a.m. on a holiday just so he could drive me to see my son. During our journey Ajay would give to me desperately needed words of encouragement all the way there and all the way back.

His wife blessed my heart, because she always had smile on her face as she waved good-bye when we pulled out of their driveway. On top of all that, when we got back to Roanoke, Ajay would always fill my gas tank up to the brim.

I will never take for granted when God's unconditional love is revealed through caring Christian friends. Going the extra mile for the sake of encouraging someone else's heart who is incarcerated or doing something special for a family member who has a loved one is prison is a tremendous blessing. Every act of kindness helped me and June through a lot of really tough times.

Even with all of the support we had, I continually longed for him to be home and I prayed for an early release; but that didn't happen. God, however, knew what I would need for my journey; and even more important - God knew what June would need. I am very thankful that God sees the big picture. June had to serve 85% of his time so that he could learn many lessons from God through His Word, and I too *(as quiet as it was kept)* was learning valuable lessons as well. One main lesson in which most people, myself included, don't do well is the issue of how to wait. Gosh! It's such an ugly little word that hangs in the balance of our microwave, give-it-to-me-now society. Nonetheless, at some point in your lives waiting on something is the inevitable journey we must all take.

On many occasions, people would ask questions about June that I did not want to answer. They had no idea how their probing questions would break my heart and cause me to feel awful, but I had to learn how to wait for God to give me His airtight answers that would close everyone's mouth. So I prayed about the main questions which were: "What did he do?" "How much time did he get?" and the last gut wrenching question which was, "When will he come home?"

But you have to hear the answers God gave me to tell them. God impressed upon my heart when they ask, "What did June do?" He said tell them, "Something that I have already forgiven;" In answer to the question of how much time he got, God said to tell them, "Too much time." And as to when will he come home? God said tell them with a smile on my face the word "**Soon**." There are no words that can describe the look on people's faces when I gave those answers, which indeed prevented any further questioning.

Then, of course, all of a sudden the conversation would be switched to a different subject. I would whisper to my heavenly Father, "Thanks, God, for equipping me with the appropriate answers so that I wouldn't feel forced to discuss his incarceration or sound like a bitter angry parent," because that really wasn't the case.

Eventually I stopped praying for early release and began to pray Father not my will, but your will be done in June's life and in my life. Then I began to catch a glimpse of this truth, that in order to create a brilliant masterpiece, it takes time, effort, and plenty of patience; but the end result will be far more valuable and worth everything you went through or are going through as you take your walk of faith. God specializes in flipping our messes over to good and glorious ministries. But it really boils down to this question:

Will I really trust God to handle the fact that my loved one is serving time in prison?

Thankfully, I finally surrendered to the point that I could say, "Yes, Lord, I trust You, because You are both capable and faithful to orchestrate my life."

God specializes in flipping our messes over to good and glorious ministries. But it really boils down to this question:

Will I really trust God to handle the fact that my loved one is serving time in prison?

Chapter 6

Close Calls

Two trips to see June in particular really stick out in my mind. They were in the winter months, and I know for sure my guardian angels were with me and prevented horrible accidents. The day of the first incident, I was traveling in light snow when I left home. As I continued, the snow got heavier moving closer to Staunton, Virginia.

I figured at that point I was almost there and I might as well continue on. I was about one mile from the facility, travelling on a very curvy road at a speed of approximately 25 to 30 m.p.h. The left side of the road was lined by a shallow ditch, and on the right side of the road there was a long two-story drop.

The snow was absolutely beautiful and I was glad that my trip was almost over. I would soon be laughing and talking with my son. All of a sudden, as I rounded the last curve in the road, the car began to slide toward the right-hand side where the long drop was located. I remember desperately saying, "Oh no, no, no!" as I quickly maneuvered the steering wheel towards the left-hand side of the road.

My attention was rudely snatched from the tranquility of the beautiful falling snow to being scared out of my wits, and my mind racing, "God help me survive!" The next thing I knew...POW! The car slid straight into the ditch on the left side of the road. And trust me I was grateful for the ditch and not the two-story drop which was the only other option on my right side.

Now while all of this was happening to me, my granddaughter, Tayonna, who was about 16 at the time was taking a nap at home, and God revealed the whole incident to her in a dream. When she woke up, she told my daughter, "Grandma is in a ditch on the side of the road and you should call her." Shone didn't believe her and insisted she had a bad dream and that I wasn't in a ditch.

However, Tayonna urgently insisted that I was in danger and tried to convince my daughter that this was more than just a dream, she described the whole thing again about me being stuck in a ditch until finally Shone spoke these words with authority, "**THE DEVIL IS A LIAR!**"

Although neither Shone nor I knew it, in the spirit realm her words cancelled the enemy's plot to take me out that day. The devil is already a defeated foe, and what

Shone spoke out of her mouth denounced the power of his attack on my life.

Okay now while that conversation was going on between Tayonna and Shone, I'm in the ditch wondering how in the world am I going to get out of this mess and back onto the slick road. I was by myself, in a rural area with no other vehicles in sight. So I sat there for a few minutes feeling shaken to the core, but I also realized I couldn't stay there long because my car was on the side of oncoming traffic even though I hadn't seen any other vehicles out there on that narrow, two-way, country road for some time.

I was cold, alone and fear was beginning to grip my heart, but I also knew better than to feed into those negative thoughts. So my plan was to carefully get out of the ditch and be on my way as soon as possible.

Suddenly I felt the peace of God engulf my very being which gave me the strength to pray these simple words, "God, please help me to get out of this ditch." Thankfully, the ditch was shallow so I pressed gently on the accelerator a few times, and the tires began to spin. Finally, I gripped the steering wheel, grabbed hold of all of the courage I could possibly muster up and hit that accelerator like I knew who I am in Jesus Christ – without too much sliding I got out and continued my journey.

I was only about 10 or 15 minutes away from the facility, and after all that I had been through to get there, the snow began to come down even harder at a rapid pace. When June finally was cleared to come into the visitation area, the first thing he said was, "Ma, what are you doing here in a snow storm?"

Good question, I thought to myself. I explained to him when I left home it was light snow, then three-quarters into the trip it began to snow harder. I followed that explanation up with the ditch story, and when I looked at his face as his head dropped between his shoulders. I knew what I had just told him did not bless him at all.

So after about a half hour had gone by, he said to me with great concern, "Ma, I really appreciate you coming, but you're traveling by yourself and it's predicted to get worst, so you better leave." Mind you this day happened before I felt the need to carry a cell phone – go figure. Now as I look back, all I can say to myself is, "Were you crazy?" Okay, so having been told to go home in the nicest way he could, I left, acknowledging he was right.

Then there was a second almost tragic trip I took to visit June on a bright, sunny, Saturday morning. I distinctly remember it was extremely cold that day, and I was by myself driving around a very curvy road at about 40 m.p.h. A car on the other side of the road blinked his headlights twice as if to warn me of something. Not knowing what was around the next curve, I took heed and slowed down to about 30 m.p.h. but that wasn't nearly slow enough.

The next thing I knew, my car slid over a large patch of ice against a mountain. When I tried to back up and straighten out, I slide to the left side and hit a guardrail which was the only thing that kept my car from going over the side of the mountain. I was nervous, scared and could clearly see that if it hadn't been for the mighty hand of God my car would have slid off the road to a fatal accident; but God is faithful and my angels were doing their job.

After a few moments I got an urgency in my spirit to quickly get out of the car and walk upward around the curve to warn other drivers my car was blocking the road. There were no vehicles in sight, but as I walked around the curve, I prayed God please send me some help.

My request was granted when I saw a tow truck slowly coming down the road. I waived at him and he was nice enough to stop. I got in his truck and his first question was, "Lady what are you doing out here in this weather?" So I explained what happened and where I was going, and asked him if he would please maneuver my car away from the guardrail so I could continue my journey.

He said he was on his way to answer a call of someone else, but he took the time to help me first – again the favor of God. As I drove a short distance very slowly towards my destination, I saw another man in the middle of the road waving at me to stop. When I rolled down my window he warned me that the roads were really bad up ahead and advised I should turn around and go back home. I agreed, but I told him that also meant I would have to travel over the same icy patch I just came off of.

He listened with an expression of concern, but assured me I could do it, and told how to get it done. After I turned my car around he said, "Listen, all you gotta do is get your speed up to about 30 m.p.h. and when you get to the icy patch take your foot off the acceleration and allow the car to glide over the ice and you'll be fine."

Well that sounded easier said than done because he couldn't hear my heart pounding like a thousand drums beating in unison; however, I did exactly what he said and of course I made it. I chuckled and took a big breathe of relief when I heard the kind gentleman yell, "You got it, you got it!!!"

Chapter 7

Blessed By Kairos Weekends

While at Augusta, June attended a Kairos Inside weekend and his description of the event was that it was extremely spiritually uplifting and powerful. A lot of healing took place in the hearts of the men who attended, including my son.

Kairos Inside is a group of ministers, deacons, and other brothers from different churches who actually go into the prisons to share with the residents the unfailing love of Jesus Christ for a weekend. Not lodging inside the prison, but going in and out for a week end. After he enjoyed the Kairos weekend so immensely, he told me about it and wanted me to attend a weekend too. At first I was a little skeptical about going, because I had never heard of Kairos Outside before. So I invited a friend to go with me and she said she would go. At the last minute, she bailed out on me. I was really disappointed, because I had to go by myself and tread upon new territory without the comfort of at least being able to share the experience each day with someone I knew.

My friend was skeptical and so was I, but I didn't tell her because I really wanted her to go with me. I couldn't convince her to change her mind and made the decision that I wouldn't judge her for not going...but I was still a little ticked with her. So what do you do when your word is on the line? Exactly! Go alone because it's critical to keep your word. I must admit though, the thought of this whole thing being a hot mess kept popping up in my mind as I continued to get ready. But finally, in spite of those negative thoughts, my bag was packed, gas in the car, directions in hand, and my 10 foot invisible wall of protection was up just in case something crazy jumped off.

When I arrived at the campsite, some very friendly women welcomed me, took my bag and showed me to my room. It's still hard to believe I was the first one to arrive but I didn't want to be late or to be the last one to arrive. I got settled and waited for everything to begin. And even though I didn't have a clue as to what the agenda would be, somehow, after getting there, I knew in my heart, that perhaps this weekend won't be so bad after all. The appearance of the atmosphere was inspiring. Every little detail showed love. The other guests arrived and the

Kairos welcoming party gave them the same beautiful greeting that I was given. I thought to myself, wow these people are really friendly – so far so good. As the weekend unfolded, to my surprise, I really had a wonderful time. I met some great people who also knew June from Kairos Inside. They bragged on him about what a great guy he was which made me feel proud, because they saw the same potentials in him I had clearly seen all along.

My weekend was filled to the brim with purpose, hit the target of where I was emotionally at that time, and allowed me to release some stuff that I didn't even know was still in my heart. In essence, the weekend was exactly what my spirit, soul, and body needed. The agenda was so well planned that I never had a chance to be bored or hungry, and the food was absolutely delicious.

I soaked up all the encouragement given to me just like a dry sponge and said goodbye to my 10 foot invisible wall of protection by the next day. The weekend helped me gain the courage to draw a line in the sand to move away from the grieving stage of my son's incarceration, pick myself up off the ground, and stop belly aching over spilled milk. Once my thinking was straightened out and on course, I began to move forward with the assurance that with God's help, I could make it through the remaining years of June's incarceration.

Kairos Outside is a safe Christian environment, made up of a group of very caring, God-fearing women from different church denominations who show the unconditional, agape love of God to mothers, wives, sisters and other female family members who have loved-ones incarcerated.

The ladies who volunteer at Kairos Outside weekends are some of the most giving, unselfish Christian women I have ever met in my life. Three of the ladies are still my good friends and we have lunch together to keep in touch. What a blessing. The group of women who volunteered their time and hard work proved to me that they genuinely had compassion about what I was going through, how I felt, and how my son's incarceration affected me and my family.

At the Kairos weekend I learned no matter how much time June had to serve, it was still only a temporary situation. I watched what I thought and the words I spoke over my son. No longer did I think of him as an inmate, but instead a resident in a correctional facility which sounded better and felt a lot better in my heart.

I had a new attitude after hearing those inspiring Talks *(otherwise known in the church world as testimonies)* from other women who survived the same thing or a different type of deep hurt in their lives that led me to know I wasn't the only one going through heartbreak. Of course we never are the only one, but the devil will inject that stupid thought into your head continuously until you realize you have the ability to kick that thought out of your head and then stand guard at the door of every thought that tries to trip you up – thank God!

When June called me after my Kairos weekend, I shared with him how much it gave me a second wind and ignited a flame of determination in my heart to be victorious until the end of his incarceration. Since these women were bold enough to share their stories, I decided to benefit from them by straightening up my back like a real soldier and share my story also. The ladies at Kairos Outside with their beautiful smiling faces and generous hearts convinced us *(the group of guests)* that we would get through this and be victorious. It's good to be reminded of God's goodness from a person who's been through the same thing you're going through. It carries more weight.

I quickly realized that the Kairos Outside volunteers gave more than met the eye to support this Kairos ministry simply because they genuinely want to be a blessing to another hurting soul who is having difficulty with their love-one's incarceration. They gave back to the community by helping someone else, and I wanted to do the same thing. Soon after my weekend, I volunteered to be a team member so I could pass on the same blessing that I received. I received the leadership training in Williamsburg, Virginia with another gal, my good friend Sue.

Then I was given the wonderful opportunity to lead two Kairos Outside weekends. One by default because the original leader was accidently injured and was unable to lead her weekend. She asked me to take her place and I agreed to step in. I was nervous because I didn't know what I was doing, but sometimes you have to lend a helping hand even when your knees are knocking. At any rate, I asked God to use me as an instrument in His hands, and He did just that. The theme, songs, menu, and everything else had already been well planned. So all I had to do was be the leader with the help of the other ladies who had organized a weekend many times before.

I remember one lady on the team, who must have sensed my anxiety, prayed for me at about 5:30 in the morning before everything got started. When the other team members realized what was going on they gathered around me and joined in the prayer for my strength and courage for the weekend. After the prayer, I knew I could do all things through Christ, and for His glory. From that point on, my team members held my hand and gave me pointers as to what to do and when to do it from beginning to the end.

On the first weekend I led by myself, at least now I had a little experience and I knew what to expect. I was responsible for a theme and I had no idea what I could use. So I prayed and asked God what should the title of my theme be? God in His infinite wisdom reminded me of one of June's testimony that he shared with me about how God held him in His arms and afterwards how he felt 100% better and was able to walk away from the window just as if he had never felt the devastation of being home sick for his family. June's personal testimony about how God embraced him gave me the theme for the Kairos Outside weekend that I was privileged to lead, which was "Wrapped In His Arms." I asked the artist to draw a female with one tear coming down her face with God's hands wrapped around her, and it was simply beautiful *(as illustrated on the next page).*

My daughter attended this weekend which was an enormous blessing for both of us. Another sister from my mother's church was there, so Shone had two familiar faces around her. Besides leading the weekend, I gave a talk on the subject "The Home Environment" which was both difficult and emotional. At one point during the talk the hurt in Shone's heart began to release in tears, and I could hear her sobbing.

I wanted to put my arms around her to give some type of comfort as a mother, but I couldn't because it was my responsibility to finish what I had written down to say. No mother wants to hear and see their daughter weep like Shone did that day, it even caused me to become emotional; but I had to pause, take a deep breath, and by the grace of God I managed to finish up. The ladies who sat near Shone gave her tissue, and no doubt prayed for her as well. Shone desperately needed a cleansing from all of the pain which encompassed the fact about her brother's incarceration and so did I.

My granddaughter Tayonna was next for a Kairos Outside weekend, but I did not serve that weekend, because at that time I was planning my wedding…ta-daah! God blesses right in the middle of a challenging situation and His timing is absolutely perfect – because God knew I would need a Holy Ghost-filled man to be an example to my son when he came home. Getting back to Tayonna, she braved her weekend alone, but not before she informed me and her mother that she appreciate the

fact that we were not going with her. Tayonna was 18 at the time, and Shone and I were preparing her to go off to college that summer. So we were kind of glad that it worked out the way it did so she could get a little taste of what it would be like to be away from home.

In hindsight, we actually accomplished two things at once, gently guiding her to go alone which was not an easy task since she had always been with us, and secondly we were helping Tayonna build her own self-confidence. Our plan worked in spite of her fears, and she had a great time. Of course, we were extremely proud of her and Tayonna was proud of herself.

Okay, now with three generations in attendance at a Kairos Outside weekend we were refreshed to know we had a support group who felt what we felt, cried just like we cried and for the same reasons – our love-one was incarcerated. After their Kairos Outside weekends, a tremendous surge of healing washed over two more generations of my family, thereby transporting us to a higher level of trust and tranquility in our Father God.

Now my daughter, my granddaughter and I can proclaim that *failure is not final*, mistakes do happen, and if we depend upon God to bring us out as winners, we will succeed every time. This truth is a process, not an overnight success, but for sure change will come.

One final word on Kairos Inside and Kairos Outside that I must mention because I would have never known anything about this ministry had they not visited Augusta Correctional Center where June spent most of his time. I was given the awesome opportunity to share my testimony at a few of the Kairos Inside "team" gatherings, which is the term used for preparing for a weekend.

I was abundantly blessed to say thanks to the male team members who sacrificed their time, efforts, and finances to prepare for each weekend going into many correctional facilities in Virginia. The ministry of Kairos Inside "gives," the residents "receive," and God gets the glory, hallelujah! I pray God's rich blessings upon the hundreds of volunteers who unselfishly give of themselves to encourage men, women, and teens who are incarcerated in many different areas.

Chapter 8

Sharing My Story at Church

On two occasions, I was asked to give my testimony about the goodness of God's love towards me and my family during the time of June's incarceration, and each time after sharing I could feel the healing process of God's love refreshing my very soul. Then another door would be opened for me to tell my story again and I appreciated each opportunity because I was reminded of just how blessed I was through the years.

As crazy as it may sound, I wish I could say I had this burning desire to write about my journey concerning my son's incarceration, but I can't because my nose would probably begin to grow, if you know what I mean. Allow me to explain. All I wanted was the "time" to pass by quickly, get it over with, and forget about the whole thing like it never happened. So going public with my story was never my intent. But God always has the best plans for us, and in October 2006 I was invited to speak on the subject of Prison Ministry in Richmond, Virginia at a Women's Conference.

The seed to write this book was planted in my heart at the conference by a precious mother in the church whom I have known for a very long time, I call her Sister Barbara. After she heard me talk about my experiences concerning June's incarceration from a parent's point of view, Sister Barbara came close to me and put a folded piece of paper in my hand and whispered in my ear *"This is not what you think it is, but you should write a book and here is the title."* When I opened the paper this is what she had written.

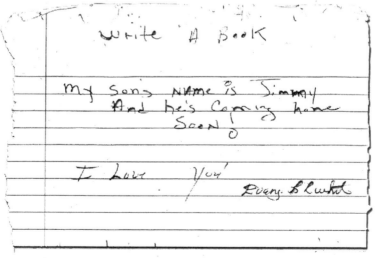

Unfortunately, I drug my feet about writing the book

for so long, the title Sister Barbara gave me was no longer closely connected to the story because June had come home. So I prayed and asked God what should I do, and He instructed me to move forward with the book, but with a different title.

Despite the fact that I left the folded piece of paper in my diary for two years, the seed did germinate and came to fruition. The rest, as they say, is history. So if this book is blessing you at all, and I pray that it will be, thank God for Sister Barbara who was willing and obedient to speak a word of wisdom to me which lit the candle to write this book. I knew it gave me joy to write letters to my family and friends but never imagined writing a book–but look at God!

I had to make a choice to accept the challenge to write this book and forget about what people may say or think about me and my family, but instead take the opportunity to hopefully bless many families by sharing my story. Every day we hear and see both positive and negative messages from the people with whom we surround ourselves. We make choices, which are our responses to these messages; however, we need to examine the choices we have made to determine if they lead us to what we were ultimately created to do with our lives; or will we allow ourselves to be shut up in a box and not live up to our true God given potential and purpose.

My sister Clem would always tell me that I should write a book, but because I could never see myself doing something like that, it sounded farfetched. Nevertheless, my sister's words became my reference point, so when Sister Barbara came along and said the same thing that was confirmation. Clem and Sister Barbara saw something I did not see about myself. There are buried treasures inside each one of us, but it's our responsibility to find them and utilize them.

Thank God for the faithful, old school mothers in the church like Sister Barbara who will yet stand bold and speak a word of wisdom and a word of knowledge into someone's life whether you like it or not; whether you can identify with it or not; and whether you receive it or not. I had to put the idea on the shelf for a minute, wrote a little bit, placed it on the shelf again, but finally after a few years I was able to go forward.

God's love, is unconditional and He will help us make the right choices. He can and will show us how to do unthinkable things that are so gigantic that we can't possibly do them by ourselves anyway, so trust God to lead and direct your path.

I know in my heart now that the only way to get on the other side of any obstacle I faced during my son's incarceration was to push through the ugly stuff—press my way to praise God and put a smile on my face—even when I didn't feel like it, then stand back and see the glory of God manifested in every direction I turned.

Facing up to the problem eliminated its power over me and God showed me how to really walk by faith and not by sight which is a daily process. Trusting God step by step is a good journey because at the end of any challenge, I always win. As proof, the scripture says *"In the Messiah, in Christ, God leads us from place to place in one perpetual victory parade."* ~ II Corinthians 2:14 (MSG)

Today, my son is without a doubt Set Free to Stay Free! No longer bound, no more chains holding him. I also believe June was not only set free physically, but the shackles were removed from his heart, his soul and his emotions. Having said that, I fully expect the best is yet to come concerning his future.

Chapter 9

The Journey Home

It was a long hard road, but finally he was transferred to Haynesville Correctional Facility, right outside of Richmond, with only 22 months left. I remember Brother Ajay telling June he wasn't going to visit him at that place next year, and June said, "Good, because I won't be here!" and we laughed. The very thought of him no longer being behind prison walls and locked behind barbwire gates sounded good to me and the thought was on the brink of being a reality.

Looking back at the whole picture now, it's amazing that I was actually rushing trying to get prepared for his arrival at the last minute. One would think I had plenty of time to get ready but if you don't pay attention to time, it can slip away from you without leaving a trace. Then June called and said he had some bad news because the computer recalculated the release date for an extra 5 days. Thank God it was 5 days and not 5 weeks or 5 months so I was okay with that.

Finally the long awaited release day came. June was more than ready to leave, blowing up my phone all morning with the same question, "did you leave yet?" My response each time was "No, but we're coming." He gladly gave away his breakfast that morning because he refused to eat another bite of prison food, so by the time we made the 3 ½ hour trip there to pick him up he was really hungry. His paperwork was done, he received a small check because he didn't have to take the Greyhound bus home, and he and the other men who were also released that day sat on the bench in front of the facility. By the time we got there, everyone else had left and he was sitting there on the bench by himself.

I imagined in my mind when this glorious day came, it would move me to tears, I would jump up and down a few times with laughter, or speak in tongues for at least 15 minutes, but instead my husband and I rolled up, June jumped in the car and we left, just like that, nothing more nothing less.

It was like he had been home all along and we were picking him up from work. That's because God redeems the time, all of the difficult puzzle pieces are in there proper places, the picture is beautiful, and nothing is missing, nothing broken, nothing lacking, only wholeness—and the family is once again "physically" together again. Praise God!

June's first question was, "Ma did you bring my clothes?" Like a magician, he quickly snatched those prison clothes off so fast it was crazy, and at the first trash can we saw June threw them away. I still remember the sweet sound of the clothes when they hit the bottom of the can. Swish! What a smash dunk victory for the "home" team! As he leaned on the back of the front seats, he asked his second question, "Where are we going to eat? I'm hungry." My husband said, "What do you have a taste for?" June said, "I don't care what it is, because anything will taste better than prison food."

We stopped at a Burger King. I can see it like it was yesterday, June leaned on the counter and asked for the biggest cheese burger they made with fries and a huge drink. We sat down and ate our first meal with June as a free man; it was so wonderful. In my heart, I needed someone to pinch me to make sure this was happening. On the outside though, I was laughing and talking - soaking it all in, thankful for God's goodness towards my son.

Now finally home and trying to settle in, June began doing construction work with my husband, but he didn't like it. So, the job search was aggressive as well as very frustrating, because when you have a checkered past it's hard to find a job. One particular evening I recall, the guys got in late and I was really tired so none of us went to church that night. In spite of that, my husband had a burning desire in his heart for us to pray together for specific things - namely June's desire for a different job, the family, etc.

Well after prayer, I began to share bits and pieces of what I went through while June was away, the good, bad and the ugly. June's eyes were glued to my face, listening without any interruption, not even one question, he and my husband just listened for about an hour with deep love in their eyes as I purged myself.

When I finally stopped talking, June said, "Ma, I've been out from behind those walls for 37 days, but tonight you just came from behind the wall." Suddenly, a serious light bulb went off in my head, because I realized the emotional pain of my son's incarceration was over for me, and I too was free. I wrote in my diary how I felt when June spoke such truth to my very soul - it was so powerful! Figuratively speaking, he led me out of my own personal captivity just like we picked him up in the car.

What an awesome God we serve. The scripture explains it best: *And ye shall know the truth, and the truth shall make (or set*) you free.* ~ John 8:32. *(*Depending upon which translation in the Bible you're reading.)* I absolutely love and appreciate how God reveals your answer through someone else who you can receive from and make it so plain even a child can understand.

As for my son, to date he has a good paying job with benefits, he is a home owner, drives a nice car, and marriage in the near future. In addition to that, I went with him to petition the court to cut his probation time in half. We didn't have the presence of an attorney or the probation officer, but we did have a good recommendation letter from the probation officer and the favor of God. Evidently, that was all we needed because his petition was granted without any objection. Thank You Jesus!

We walked out extremely relieved, but I took notice no one else was entering or exiting the Courthouse when we came out. Not even one attorney going over last minute strategies with his client. It was like God gave us a private moment to reflect and relish in June's victory.

I was so happy for him I twirled around a couple times in front of the Courthouse and danced a little bit. June looked at me and said, "Ma, if you gotta dance, then go on and dance." I danced in front of the window where he was detained until the guards took him away with his hands and feet in chains. Oooh, but not this time!!! He and I both walked away free, laughing and giving God praise. As you can imagine, that was one of the best days of my life.

Today, my son is without a doubt Set Free to Stay Free! No longer bound, no more chains holding him. I also believe June was not only set free physically, but the shackles were removed from his heart, his soul and his emotions. Having said that, I fully expect the best is yet to come concerning his future. Just like the story of Joseph in the Bible who went from prison to the palace in a high position for a set time, for the sole purpose to deliver his whole family from famine.

None of our struggles, tears and heartache is ever wasted - they grow us up, make us strong and courageous which in turn gives us a strong testimony to help someone else…you can make it! Don't give up on yourself, not now – not ever.

I will close my story on this note, if you are going through a similar situation wherein your loved-one is already incarcerated or you're faced with the possibility that the same might happen, my prayer is that you will trust God for it all. He will definitely see you through any challenge. **Shalom**…

Numbers 6:24-26

The Lord bless thee, and keep thee:

The Lord make His face shine upon thee,

And be gracious unto thee;

The Lord lift up His countenance upon thee,

*and give thee **peace**.*

About The Author

Jean West is retired after more than 35 years of being a legal assistant. Additionally, she is a cancer survivor since 2013 – to God be the glory! She is married to a wonderful God-fearing man, and they maintain a healthy God-centered relationship. Two incredible children, and three beautiful grandchildren – they make her heart smile. She enjoys teaching adult Sunday School, as well as being an assistant for her pastor's wife. Currently, she appreciates the opportunity to work with We Care Prison Ministry at her church, wherein she writes a monthly letter to residents who are incarcerated in Virginia and other locations. She can be reached at beautifulproverbs@gmail.com.

Made in the USA
Charleston, SC
28 April 2016